Ta

Preface — page 4

Introduction — page 6

Chapter 1 — page 10

Why a Container Home

Chapter 2 — page 19

Site Selection

Chapter 3 — page 29

Getting Your Containers

Chapter 4 — page 36

Arrange for the Excavation

Chapter 5 — page 42

Site Preparation

Chapter 6 — page 46

Timing is Everything

Chapter 7 — page 52

It's Time to Dig!

Chapter 8   page 58

    Filling in the Sides

Chapter 9   page 62

    The Retaining Wall

Chapter 10   page 65

    Preparing to Pour the Slab

Chapter 11   page 78

    Framing Walls and Partitions

Chapter 12   page 90

    Preparation to Bring the Dirt Back Over

Chapter 13   page 95

    Plumbing Considerations

Chapter 14   page 105

    Electrical Considerations

Chapter 15   page 113

    Cabinets and Cabinet Walls

Chapter 16   page 120

    Flooring

Chapter 17   page 124

    A Porch Roof

Chapter 18   page 128

    Ventilation

Chapter 19   page 133

    Wood Stoves and Heating

Chapter 20   page 138

    Off-Grid Considerations

Chapter 21   page 144

    Well and Water System

Chapter 22   page 152

    Agriculture

Chapter 23   page 158

    Final Thoughts

Off the Grid and Underground

How to Build a Storage Container House Underground

Preface:

As we begin this book, it is our objective to try and take you through the process of constructing a container home in a step by step manner from beginning through completion. We will endeavor to keep the process orderly and flowing so that you will have as few problems as possible by following the guidelines. Of course, there will be additions and deletions that you may bring to the table, but we believe that if you review this book before you start and take these steps into account as you plan, the end product will suit your needs admirably.

We will not detail everything. For example, we suggest that you pour a 6 inch cement slab over the top of the containers. We will not detail how to pour cement or do concrete finish work. We will assume (could be dangerous) that either you have sufficient experience in pouring concrete or that you will have someone present, either friend or paid worker/contractor that can supply that knowledge and equipment. The same goes for excavation, carpentry, plumbing, and electrical. We find that many people who consider this type of construction are already "do-it-yourselfers" with multiple skills. Even then, getting help is always nice!

We have tried to give you the benefit of our experience by including some things that worked really well and some things that did not work so well. We also will list some things that we would do differently should we have the opportunity to build another similar structure. There are also a few improvements in materials since we built our home that we believe will give you a better result. In the end, we cannot guarantee your results, but it is our hope that we can help you make some good choices.

Introduction:

We have been interested in non-conventional building techniques for some time and have explored many different options through the years. In the summer of 2007 we began a journey that would lead us to one of the most unconventional homes we have ever experienced. We were already living off-grid and were searching out ways of keeping our carbon footprint way below the national average. We were not completely altruistic in this quest either, since we were also guided by the practical considerations of keeping our energy and operating costs as low as possible.

Having seen a few homes built by tunneling into the mountainsides of Napa and Sonoma valleys in California, as well as wine storage caves, we were very impressed by the constant temperature qualities of underground structures but not so impressed with the costs of the same. So we began to research how we could build underground with as limited as possible cash outlay.

While reading a book called, "Dare to Prepare" by Holly Deyo, we noted some plans for a makeshift bomb shelter constructed from a cargo container. There were not a lot of details, but the idea stuck with us and plans began to develop in our minds and then onto paper. Over the course of the following year, those plans grew into the reality of our home built of two forty foot long cargo containers inserted into the southern slope of our property in Northern California.

We did not realize at first how much interest there would be in this unusual home. We were just very happy with how well the concept worked. With 100+ degree temperatures outside, the inside of our home never got above 80-82 degrees. If we were better about closing off the solar tubes and had heavy insulated curtains for the front windows and doors, it would be even more remarkable. During the 20 degree nights of mid-winter, the inside temperature does not go below 62 degrees without any heater on, and it is easy to bring that temperature up with a small RV catalytic heater. This means we have no air-conditioning costs and very little heating costs throughout the year. Even though there is a substantial savings of cost per square foot in building with this technique, the real cost savings are ongoing through this energy savings on a monthly basis; and it will get even more notable as energy costs continue to rise.

As we shared the idea with friends and people would visit us and remark on the unique qualities of our home, we began to understand that maybe we had ahold of a concept that needed to be shared. Finally at the prompting of our older son, we decided to write this book and share with you the process we engaged in building this unique home.

We hope you will be stimulated by this presentation and should you decide to go ahead with constructing your own masterpiece, we would be glad to try and answer any questions you might have. Enjoy the journey.

Steve Rees

Chapter 1

Why a Container Home

Why would anyone in their right mind want to chuck conventional wisdom and building techniques in order to build a home out of recycled shipping containers? After all, only Hobbits live underground and they have big feet – right?

Actually, the reasons for using cargo containers to construct an underground dwelling are not as strange as it might seem on passing glance. The cost of construction is one reason that makes them attractive. Our two container dwelling or 640 square feet of floor space cost right at $30,000 fully finished. That is less than $50 per square foot which is less than one half of the conventional costs for construction at the time of this writing. A livable space could be done for even less and a lot could be saved using recycled materials.

Another aspect of cost is how much money will be saved monthly on energy costs both in summer and in winter. This savings will add up over the years to make this style of living almost start to pay you, there will be so much savings. This really is the deal maker for really seriously looking at this style of living. We are off-grid and all our energy is solar or generator so this minimized demand for energy consumption really adds up quickly. People walk into our home in the summer and can't believe we don't have an air-conditioner running up a big power bill. It is very comfortable.

A second consideration is the ease and speed of this style of building. In our own experience we were "livable", start to finish, in less than three months. Times will vary per individual according to level of finish required and amount of help available, but it seemed to us to be a very short route to permanent living space.

This brings up another point. This really is a permanent structure. It is buried in the ground, wisely out of any flood plain (more on that later) with a concrete slab and dirt on top. It's not moving anywhere and nothing is going to make it change its mind. You don't even have to worry about a tree falling on the roof. We had a D-4 Caterpillar running around on top of the roof leveling out the final dirt covering – not a dent. You also do not have to worry about bad weather destruction like hurricanes or tornados because it is underground like a storm cellar; a very nice comfortable storm shelter.

It can also double up as a bomb shelter, depending on how you engineer the structure and closures and air venting/filtration systems. If you keep the front steel doors closable, they can help protect against blasts and at about 3 feet of earth coverage over the top, most radiation is stopped. Two to three feet of water can also shield against radiation so water barrels stacked in front can help shield as well as the dirt on the top. I am only mentioning these ideas as an aside. Please don't think of this structure only in terms of a bomb shelter. It can be so much more than that. These are excellent side benefits, but the real benefits come from living in this space as your home.

Note the Container Doors still intact.

Another benefit is that this style of building can really help to keep your tax base lower than normal.

Depending on how your jurisdiction treats this form of dwelling, the savings can be significant. We will deal with the planning department in an upcoming section. Since this is a non-conventional style of building, you have to be very careful on how you approach your planning department. Just the fact that you are paying less per square foot will keep your assessment lower, even if you have to show your receipts.

One of the really true attractions of this style of home is its incredible use of the thermal mass of the earth surrounding it for constant temperature control summer and winter with minimal energy input. In California, we can get up to 110 degrees outside in mid-summer. During that outside temperature, we don't get over 82 degrees inside with no air-conditioner. Sometimes we use a fan to circulate the air, but that takes little energy.
It is the thermal mass quality of the earth that makes that possible.

During the winter we can have a cold snap into the 20's but the temperature inside will not go below 63 degrees even without a heater. That also is a result of the thermal mass quality of the earth. The earth is so big that it doesn't change its temperature too much; actually just a few degrees either way from summer to winter. The surface of the earth is the only area that is subject to temperature swings. Once you get a couple of feet below the surface, the thermal mass effect takes over and there is very little temperature differential from summer to winter. The earth constant is usually between 55 and 60 degrees. If you are warmer than the earth core temperature, it will "suck" the temperature away from you to get you down to the core temperature. If you are cooler than the core temperature, it will give you "heat" to get you up to the core temperature. That is why you need to put some insulation on the outside of the containers so that you can maintain the temperature without losing it to the temperature of the earth surrounding the home. The thermal mass works for you in the summer and against you in the winter, but the insulation helps even those swings out.

It is interesting to note that many of the early history "root cellars" were made to take advantage of this thermal mass characteristic of the earth. Before refrigeration was available, the root cellar kept food preserved for much longer periods because it was able to protect against the summer heat and the winter freeze. We're just expanding on the same principle.

The container building technique is also a very earth friendly type of structure for several reasons. As already mentioned regarding the low energy requirements for heating and cooling; obviously this vastly reduces the carbon footprint for the occupants of this type of structure. It is also a very non-obtrusive format that does not dominate the landscape.

See the wildflowers growing on the roof!

A person can be standing within 50 feet of our home and not even know it is there from many angles. When you do see it, it blends into the surroundings quite readily. We also used local stone for the retaining walls so that it blends in even more. Landscaping could even be designed so that the entrance would be concealed by properly placed vegetation.

Another benefit of having a home underground is that it really brings down the noise level. We have had many times when a lot of noise is going on outside and we never heard a thing. Even if the dogs bark when someone comes onto our place, we have really got to listen to hear them. When storms are going on, we get some noise in the solar light tubes and we can hear rain pitter pat on the prism lenses, but it is not nearly as obtrusive as the normal noise levels of a conventional structure. I can just imagine that this type of structure would make an excellent sound recording studio. I'll have to try it sometime.

Chapter 2

Site Selection

One of the advantages of our property is that it has a south facing gentle slope. To some, this is a disadvantage because they are looking for flat "bottom land" that is easy to till and usually more fertile. This may be true, but there are some offsetting advantages to a sloped land as well.

One strong advantage is that you have good drainage away from the structure. Even in the middle of winter with daily downpours of rain, it is very easy to ensure adequate drainage by taking advantage of the sloping away from the structure. There is no tendency for water to collect as long as the drainage is properly installed. Water goes down, and down is away from the structure. We are also a good elevation above any stream bed or flood plain so there is no issue with water backing up to cover any part of the structure.

We installed 18" of drain gravel all around the sides of the containers and 6" under them with drain pipes installed so that the overall effect is a giant "French Drain" that functions very efficiently. We have not had any problems with any water pooling around the containers even while rain had been pouring down for weeks as it does in California during our monsoon season. I have seen some areas as we have travelled in the USA that would not work well for this type of structure. There are some areas that are very flat with high water tables and drainage would not happen under these circumstances. Carefully examine your proposed site to make sure that you can ensure adequate drainage at all times of the year.

Having said that, we have a friend in Texas that found a large earth moving company that had a bunch of old tires from the big tractors and they were willing to bring them out to his place. He stacked them with a tractor, and then filled them with dirt and formed them around his structure so that they made a "U" shaped wall that bermed around 3 of the sides. It wasn't quite as efficient as what we have done here, but it was way better than not doing anything. Keep your thinking cap on. You may be able to come up with a design that will still work for your area of the country.

Another thought I have had is to just bring the soil up over the containers in much the same way that ammunition bunkers are built in military installations on flat ground. There is no rule that says how to get the dirt over the top, be inventive.

If drainage was the problem with a high water table, you could even build a drain field with gravel to set the containers on and then place tires around the sides with gravel in between the container and tires for a drain field and then bring dirt over the top. You could even pour cement pads to elevate the container above expected water levels. Of course this would all add expense to the project, but I suspect that there are extra expenses already expected from the environment you would be building in. It could still work.

We also selected our site to optimize the collection of solar energy both passive and active. Our slope faces south which I believe is perfect. This allows you to set your solar panels for electricity within easy distance of the house. It also allows you to take advantage, especially in the winter, of the warming rays of the sun as it hits the front of the structure in the middle of the day. We planned our dwelling to be off grid, so it was important for us to be able to maximize these solar benefits. The light gathering capacity of this orientation is also important as it keeps a cheery level of light coming in the windows even on a stormy day.

In conjunction with this comes also the consideration of where to allow trees to stay and which need to come out so that the light is optimized and yet not too strong in the summer months. Also the type of trees is a consideration. We have Oak trees in our front area which works rather well since they have leaves on them in the summer that give shade and then the leaves drop off in the fall and allow the suns warmth to come through and give us the passive solar benefits. We also built on a porch roof that is angled to help give shade in the summer, but allow the sun rays to hit the front of the structure during the winter months when the suns angle to the earth is much lower than in the summer.

Oak Trees for Summer Shade.

It is very important to draw up a carefully measured plot plan and floor plan before you get started with the actual building. You will need accurate measurements as you begin to install the drain and sewer lines and plan your distances from the various other installations (water, electricity, gas, etc.) you will need to connect with. Make sure you draw everything to scale so that the measurements will be very close and no mistakes made. After the containers are in place and you are going about making holes in the floor to bring up the plumbing and water, you don't want to make too big or too many holes to find where the pipes are. Good measurements make for good installations.

It has been said many times that if you fail to have a plan, then you have a plan to fail. You may not totally fail, but you will have a lot of headaches if these things are not carefully placed on paper before you begin. The plans don't have to be professionally drawn up. You can do them yourself if you take the time to draw them on larger sheets of paper and draw them to a scale (such as ¼ inch on the paper = 1 foot in reality) so that there is a reasonable representation on the paper that helps you visualize what the structure is going to look like when it is finished.

Another consideration is the stability of the soil you are working with. A blessing to our property is the nature of our soil. It is mostly shallow (6-8 inches) before it starts turning into heavy gravel, then transitioning into decomposed granite/rock for quite a depth. This makes a very stable when digging out the trench to place the containers in. The soil remained in place without caving in or sloughing off as the containers were placed and the drain gravel inserted for the "French Drain".

If you have sandy soil, that could be a problem. I'm sure you could talk with a local dirt work contractor and determine a way to cope with such a soil. It may be more expensive or take more time or more equipment. Another problem would also be heavy layers of stone, like a limestone cap. This could also be worked through, but again would require more equipment and planning.

A shifting soil may also need to have some type of foundation or pylons placed to ensure that the containers do not shift after placement. Our soil was stable enough that it did not require any more prep than a 6 inch layer of gravel to facilitate drainage. These containers have not moved at all since their placement. Be sure you have the stability situation well understood before you begin the project.

Another aspect of your site selection will also depend on how you want to apply the features of your home. If you are depending on it to be part home and part bunker protection, you may want to select the site to be more secluded, and possibly protected by a close ridge in the direction of any perceived threat. If you want extreme privacy, you may want to keep the site closer to land features that offer more protection and seclusion. Rock outcroppings, trees, or carefully planned landscaping can all serve to help conceal the exposure of your structure to the casual onlooker.

Of course you will want to keep your home accessible yet private, so your road into the structure will have to be planned so that it doesn't cause erosion through heavy use, yet it brings your vehicle in close enough to the home for ease of carrying things in and out.

You will also need to make sure there is enough slope so that if you are equipping your home with a septic tank and leach line system, there is enough slope and room on your property to install these with the proper slopes and distances.

You will also need to make sure how you are going to bring the other sources for hookups to your structure. How is the water going to come into the structure? Will you bring it through the roof or through the floor? The same goes for the electric and gas/propane – roof or floor? If you are going to use solar, are you going to collect the electricity at one area of your property and bring it by wire to your home, or are you going to mount the panels on the structure and have the inverters and batteries installed into the structure? These are all planning aspects that need to be decided before you begin the project.

Chapter 3

Getting Your Containers

Now that you have your site selected, your measurements carefully marked out on paper, and your plot design in place, the next step is to find and purchase your containers. Depending on where you live containers could be just around the corner, or require a major distance of "Drayage" to be delivered to your site. In our case, we were able to locate a container reseller near the Port of Oakland, California, and purchase our containers from him. We were able to hire him to deliver the containers as well. His method of delivery was a 4-wheel drive pickup pulling a 40 foot gooseneck trailer with a tilt bed. This gave him the ability to drop the container virtually any place we chose. The containers are about #7000 empty, so this is very doable.

Containers being delivered

It is good to shop around. There are usually several outlets around a port area. Even inland there are many options since containers are shipped by train and truck to facilities around the country. At the time of this writing, there is a high level of competition because international shipping has slowed way down due to the economic conditions and containers are being offered at quite low rates just to empty out the storage space because of the excessive backlog. Now should be a good time to make a good deal.

Another aspect of determining your price is to make sure the company can deliver your container so you don't have to hire some other company to do it. Usually a package deal gives you better costs rather than using several different companies.

It is also good to find a company that has the ability to paint the containers with more protective coats of paint and prepare them to be placed underground. The company we used was able to give us 3 coats of Navy grade paint so that our containers were well covered and protected from rust for a good period of time. They also let us inspect the containers and chose ones that suited our inspection for dents and welds and skin repairs. If they won't work with you to let you pick good containers and help you get them well painted, then find someone who will. There is usually enough competition out there to find a company that will help you get what you want.

We bought 2 – 20 foot containers for other storage, and found out that we could also get them sprayed with insulating foam to help keep them cooler inside, or warmer in the winter.

This is an option you may want to consider. If you do, consider in the planning stage what walls you want to have furred out and maybe have these boards in place before the spraying in of the insulation. Otherwise, you will have to peel off the insulation in the areas that you want to place the boards once it comes time to install them. I have found the foam to be quite effective, so you may want to consider this option and find a company that can do the foam as part of the preparation of your container before it ships out to your building site.

Our 40 foot containers cost us approximately $2,000 each plus another $500 each for the delivery. That was in 2008 dollars. It was also before the global shipping slowdown, so today's pricing may actually be quite similar. This pricing included the extra paint and any dent repair required. We decided to use 2 containers for our living space requirements. You could easily expand on this idea and use 3, 4 or more. The 640 square feet that these 2 containers provided have proven to be adequate for our needs. I would challenge you to learn how to minimize your space requirements and live more simply. That is part of what off grid living is all about in my books.

We found that there are several options when it comes to purchasing a container. The standard container is a 40 foot container that is 8 feet high and 8 feet wide. These also come in 20 foot lengths and I have seen up to 53 foot lengths on trucks. This might present an issue in getting the delivery to your property. There is also a 40 foot "high cube" that is an extra 18 inches taller than the standard 8 foot wall. This is what we used since we decided that it would be nicer to have that extra 18 inches overhead to build extra storage and not feel like the roof was caving in on us. There are many times when we are really glad to have that extra room overhead. I have seen a few other lengths, some shorter than 20 foot even, but the main ones are 20 and 40 footers.

I have observed containers for sale in most classified sections of most area newspapers. I have seen them being offered on Craig's List and E-Bay on the internet. I have also seen quite a few sitting by the side of the road with a "For Sale" sign and phone number painted on them. I have seen storage yards filled with stacks of containers. I believe that finding a container is the least of your worries. If you let people know that you are looking for containers to buy, they will come out of the woodwork I'm sure.

Mostly you want to find one that has minimal to no rust; minimal to no dents. You want to make sure the doors are in good working order, and that they are capable of being locked if need be. Even if you don't want to use these doors to lock with after you have moved in, it may be handy to be able to use them to lock up your equipment while you are in the building phase. Also inspect the floor to make sure it doesn't have too big of gouges in it. You may want to sand and finish these floors for a final surface instead of spending a lot of extra money to purchase floor coverings. We'll talk more about that later.

When you have your containers delivered, have them placed as close to the installation site as possible without getting in the way of the excavation. Talk with your excavation contractor about where that should be. It is good to have the containers on site before starting the digging so that there is no lag time for placing the containers into the hole once the excavator has prepared the site. For the excavating contractor, time is money and they do not want to tie up there big equipment any longer than necessary before they move it onto the next job site. Try and have as much in place as possible so that there is little if any wasted time. Usually any wasted time on their part is going to end up being wasted money on your part. Use good planning and good material preparations.

Chapter 4

Arrange for the Excavation

You are now ready to find an excavation contractor to dig the trench to place your containers into. Have them come out to the site so that they can see what you are really asking them to do. Let them give you their input and suggestions as well. A good contractor has been doing dirt work for a long time and their experience is invaluable. We learned later on that our contractor actually gave us a low bid because he was so intrigued by the idea of the project and he had many ideas and pointers along the way that saved us much time and trouble.

Make sure they give you a firm quote in writing so that you lock in your costs. If they are supplying the drain gravel, make sure that is in the quote. If you are buying the gravel from another source (which we did) make sure you know how much gravel that is going to be and how much that is going to cost along side of the excavation costs. As I mentioned earlier, make sure they tell you where to put the containers so they are out of the way for the beginning of the digging.

It is a plus to make sure the contractor has laser leveling equipment so that the grade for the containers can be precise. Our contractor had this equipment and it made the installation so much better. When the containers were placed side by side and the gravel was placed around them, they were exactly level and you could barely slip a piece of paper in between them. Our contractor performed par excellent!

The laser equipment also allowed our contractor to place a ¼ inch to each foot slope in the floor of the trench and then bring in the drain gravel level so that it helped to facilitate the drainage of any water away from the containers but allowed them to set exactly level. This was one of the contractor's ideas that I would not have thought of. It has proven over time to work out very well.

Make sure that the contractor plans well for how deep to dig the trench so that when the dirt is brought back over the top of the containers it will be at least 3 feet deep. This will involve considering the slope of the land and calculating how far back the trench will have to be to get to that depth. Also make sure they are allowing for the extra width needed to install the drain gravel around the sides and back of the container. I wanted to make sure there was plenty of drainage so we decided on 18 inches extra space for the drain rock to fill into. We added an extra 4 inches as well to allow for the Poly-styrene board insulation that we used. This gave us the width of the containers plus an extra 22 inches on each side, or 44 inches total extra for the complete width of the trench.

Make sure the quote also includes the trench to the septic tank and the hook-up to the septic system. Optimally, you should have the septic system already in place. If you end up using the same contractor for your septic system as you do for the containers, you might save some money with a package deal because their equipment would already be on site so transportation costs and time could be saved. In our case, we had already installed our septic system several years earlier so we just included the hook-up in our bid.

Also make sure the quote includes the contractor filling in the dirt back over the top of the containers and smoothing out the dirt with a final finish grade. This should also include finishing the grade of the driveway that will come up to the container. You want to make sure that when the contractor pulls their equipment from your site, you have a pleasing appearance and function of your site.

Make sure that the contractor you use has equipment adequate enough to also place the containers once the trench is in place. If they cannot lift the containers into place, then you will have to arrange for a crane or lift which will be extra time and money. Our contractor was able to take off the bucket of his excavator and attach cables to each corner of the container and lift the containers right over into the trench when it was ready. It worked really well.

If there are any grades that you need to cut for the landscaping, make sure this is included into the quote. It is much easier and more cost effective to get all this work done while the equipment is on site rather than bringing them back later.

Make sure you have asked around about the reputation of the contractor you use. Unfortunately in the construction business, there are some "fly-by-night" individuals out there who will give you a good quote but not hold to it or get part of the work done and then leave. You want to make sure you use someone well established in the community that people will not hesitate to recommend. Our contractor was good to his word throughout the whole project. At the end he told me that if I needed to do another project of this scope he would have to bid it a little higher because his fuel costs had been more than he had planned. He took the financial burden and kept to his quote with me rather than raise his rate. That's the kind of people I like to work with!

Chapter 5

Site Preparation

The first thing we did to prepare the site for excavation was to mark out corner stakes and paint lines where the dirt was to be dug. This did several things. First of all, it gave us a clear visualization of where the containers were going to go so that if we wanted to make any changes, now was the time. It also helped to identify which trees needed to come out either because they were where the digging was to take place, or they were in the way of the tractor as it did the digging. Our trees were fairly small, so the excavator asked us to leave them in place so that he could grab them with his bucket and get them out of the way including the roots. He had them out in no time when he started the digging work.

At this point it is important to determine the exact slope so that you can calculate the exact distance and depth needed to properly place the containers so that they will have enough dirt over the top when you are finished. We took a 10 foot board with a level on top and ran it perpendicular to the slope keeping it level. Then we measured from the end of the board down to the ground. These numbers can be entered into an equation to give you the slope of the land. For example, if the measurements were 6 inches from the board to the ground then the slope would be ½ foot per 10 feet or .5 divided by 10 which equals a 5% grade.

For a 40 foot container with a 5% slope That would give you 40 X .05 = 2 which means that you would need to dig 2 feet in the back and nothing in the front to have the container level. Now if you need the high cube container which is 9 feet 6 inches tall to be deep enough in the ground to have 8 inches of isolation plus 6 inches of concrete plus 3 feet of dirt you now need to dig the trench deep enough to account for all these. This would be 9 feet 6 inches plus 8 inches plus 6 inches plus 3 feet. All of these equal 13 feet 8 inches. This is the depth of the trench at the back coming level out to the front. By the way, you also want to allow for 6 inches of gravel under the container so now your hole is 14 feet 2 inches.

I recommend that you also have your excavator put a ¼ inch to a foot drop on the floor of the trench and then level the gravel starting at 6 inches at the back increasing just enough to keep level as you come forward. This will help to facilitate drainage off of the pad that the containers are sitting on. This was suggested to us by our excavator and it has worked out very well.

As you mark out the corners, be sure that they are square so the trench is dug square. If you measure from one corner to the opposite diagonal corner and then do the same for the two corners left, these measurements should be the same. If they are not the same, then adjust the position of two corners on the same side and re-measure until you get the same measurement on each diagonal. You want to start out square otherwise you will have no end of headaches.

Once you have the stakes in place and your slope calculated and your depth determined, go over these numbers and placements with your excavator and make sure you calculations are correct and that the excavator knows and understands what they are about to do. You can never be too sure about your calculations. Remember, measure twice (or more) and cut once! This works here too.

Chapter 6

Timing is Everything

Once the plans are drawn, the stakes are in place and everyone is on the same page, it's time to start gathering the various components that will make this a successful project. It is important to have everything in place before you start otherwise there will be delays that will cost time and money.

The first thing I recommend that you get on site is the containers themselves. You want to have them present so you can begin visualizing the space you are going to have to work with. It is important to use a chalk line and measure out and mark where the walls and partitions are going to go. You also want to draw in where you are going to put the plumbing fixtures and drains. If these are all drawn out ahead, it is easy to take off the measurements when you are installing the drain system and any other utilities you are bringing up through the floor.

It is also very good to get these drawn in so that you can begin to see how much space you are going to have and how you want to arrange this space most efficiently. We used a permanent marker pen once we had everything decided and agreed upon so that when it came time to place the walls and partitions, it was easy to bring them to the marks.

Arrange for the drain gravel to be placed close to the project. Using the excavations contractor's estimates, have that much brought out and sitting in a pile ready to install and maybe have a little extra just in case. You can always use the extra on the driveway are.

We started arranging for the Poly Styrene board quite a bit in advance because it was manufactured on the east coast and had to be trucked to our location. There were several changes of hands in the process so it took some time from when we placed the order to when we actually had the sheets on site. Give yourself some time to get this done.

Another item that you will need to acquire ahead of time is the "erosion fabric" that you will use to place between the drain gravel and the dirt on the sides of the trench. This fabric keeps the dirt separated from the gravel so that the gravel stays clean and functioning properly for drainage. This fabric usually comes in large roles and we found it locally at a landscape supply yard.

Poly Styrene sheeting just after Delivery

If you are not pressed for time on the start of your project, you could save some money by waiting until your excavation contractor has his equipment close to your site on another project and can quickly come across to your site. We were able to work with our contractor in this way and it helped him give us a lower bid.

Other supplies you should have on hand are whatever pipes you are going to bury under the containers. Sewer pipe, water pipe, electric conduit, drain pipe, or even gas pipe. Once the digging starts it is amazing how quickly you can get to this phase and if you have to pull off the job just to go get the supplies, it can cost you money while the contractor idles his machinery to wait for you to get back. Be Ready!

Placing sewer and drain lines

Another preparation you can have in place is to talk with the concrete supplier so that you know how much lead time they need to send out a load of concrete. Also along with that, if you are going to use a concrete pump (and I highly recommend that you do) you will need to know how much lead time they will need too.

One more area of preparation is to have the framing material on hand because you will want to use it to build a support for the middle of the containers as you pour the slab on the top. This will help to keep the center of the roofs from sagging. I will talk a little more about this as we get to that stage.

Chapter 7

It's Time to Dig!

Now comes the moment you have been waiting for. You have made your preparations, the contractor is on site and your first scoop of dirt comes out of the ground. Hopefully by now, your lines on the ground reflect that you have allowed and extra 22 inches on each side of the containers for 18 inches of gravel plus 4 inches of insulation. As the excavator goes down in the soil, keep measuring to make sure you are keeping that distance so that the walls do not angle in as you go down. Frequent measurements will help keep everything on track.

According to your calculations for the slope of your ground and the depth needed to have at least 3 feet of soil come back over the container plus the slab plus the insulation plus the 6 inches of gravel to set on, you will have the excavator keep digging until you have reached this depth in the back of the trench. From this depth in the back, the excavator should level off out to the front of the trench with a ¼ inch per foot drop to facilitate drainage of surface water.

Another thing I would mention here is that as we were digging, I kept culling out the large rocks that were dug up by the excavator. My purpose was to assemble a large collection of stones that I could later use to erect the retaining walls that help keep the soil and drain rock back around the sides of the containers. You may elect to just form up these retaining walls with concrete and forgo the "rock picking" but there could also be other uses for these rocks. If you have to buy them, they can be pricey.

Impressive Pile!

Before putting the drain gravel on the bottom of the excavation, dig the ditches to accommodate the sewer, the water, the electric, gas, and the drain pipe. These should be installed and covered before the gravel is placed for the containers to sit on. Make sure the stub-ups measure out to your floor plan using the placement of the back of the container as your measuring point and your floor plan for accurate measurement. Later when you go to hook up your sewer, you will be able to measure to the stub-up site and cut a small hole in the floor and come within a few inches for hook-up.

Once these are all covered, it's time to place the gravel for drainage under the containers as well as a stable platform for the containers to set on and remain level. The gravel should be 6 inches deep at the back of the trench and then leveled with a laser as it comes out to the front. The front gravel depth will be a little more than the back because of the ¼ inch per foot slope the excavator cut into the bottom of the trench. Once this gravel is leveled out, everything is ready to place the containers into the trench.

We were able to use the excavator to pick up the containers by taking the bucket off the excavator and attaching a cable to each corner of the container leading up to a large "U-bolt" connected to the arm of the excavator. We had to measure and get the cables made with loops at each end at a local cable manufacturer. At the time it cost about $125 which wasn't bad instead of hiring a crane to come out and do the job.

In placing the containers into the trench, it is important to measure the distance from the side of container on each side to the side of the trench so that you make sure you have equal distance and insure that the containers are in the exact center. While the containers or suspended on the cables connected to the excavator, they move quite easily by having a rope tied to one of the corners.

In placing the containers make sure they are as close to each other as possible. Once you start to fill in the sides with drain gravel, the weight of the gravel will actually push them even more together. When ours were finished, you could hardly fit a piece of paper in between them. The laser leveling had them both sitting so well that there was virtually no difference in elevation between either on. Our excavator new his business and it really showed.

Chapter 8

Filling in the Sides

Now that the containers are set in place, it is time to begin filling in the sides and back with the drain gravel. It is important to fill in equal amounts on each side as you go up the side. We started filling with just one container in place and everything was going along just fine until as one tractor bucket was being dumped in, I noticed the container move slightly from the pressure of the weight of the gravel against its side. We immediately stopped filling and placed the other container on the other side and began to fill from that side until we were at equal depth on both sides. You live and learn!

We anchored the ground barrier fabric onto the dirt bank to help keep it from falling into the open trench, but even so as the gravel was poured in the fabric pulled away from the anchors and had to be held in place. It is best to wear some type of face mask at this point as the dust from the gravel is stifling! The key is to get the landscape fabric to stay up on the dirt side of the trench while making sure the Poly Styrene panels are secure up against the outside of the container while the drain gravel is poured into the open space. Once the bottom is filled with the gravel, this tends to push the panels securely against the container helping to keep everything in place.

Holding the Poly Styrene board up while the gravel fills.

Keep evenly filling up the sides and back with drain gravel until you are level with the top of the container. As we found out, It is best to have the front of the container retaining walls built before you start filling with drain gravel. If you don't have these in place you will not be able to fill all the way to the top in the front of the containers as there will be nothing to hold back the drain gravel and it will spill out the front of the sides.

Bring the gravel up all around the back and sides so that the top of the container and the top of the gravel are at the same level. Our containers are 9' 6" inches tall so we cut the extra needed amount, plus an additional 6" out of another sheet of Poly Styrene to bring it up to the top.

The extra 6 inches became the form that we poured the slab against. We backfilled against the Poly Styrene panels with more gravel so that the gravel actually came up to the top of the panels giving it the strength needed to withstand the force of the concrete pour.

With the excavation equipment on site, we worked quickly and diligently to get the retaining walls up as fast as possible so we could get the gravel filled in thoroughly all around the sides. Fortunately, the contractor had another job going so we were able to get it done and not hold him up. By the end of the day, with both containers in place and as much gravel as we could place before it started spilling out, we looked like this.

Chapter 9

The Retaining Wall

In order to be able to fill in the gravel around the front part of the sides, without the gravel spilling out in front of the container, it is necessary to construct a retaining wall. In our case, we elected to build it out of the stone that we collected from the excavation of the trench. In hind sight, I would strongly recommend forming up the retaining walls and pouring them with cement reinforced with steel.

Having said that, we began to build up our walls with concrete and stone, sealing off the openings that were beside the containers so that once these retaining walls were in place, we could pour in the rest of the gravel that would fill up to the wall but not go any further. We used the larger stones on the bottom with a wider base, and then built up to where the top of the dirt at the side of the container allowed us to begin to stretch the retaining wall out laterally. This was necessary for later when we would bring the dirt back over the top of the container, holding back the dirt from spilling down onto the front of the containers.

Building a rock/cement retaining wall

It took several days because we could only go so high with the stones and concrete before they would threaten to collapse before the concrete set up. Try and make sure you have a solid base for the structure to stand on so that later when you pile the dirt and gravel against it from the other side, it remains stable. Another need for this strength is that when it is raining and the ground gets saturated, it gets heavier too. We will talk more about that when we talk about covering the containers back up with the dirt on top.

Another thing that I would mention if you are going to use stone, make sure the stones you are using are going to remain stable. Different types of stone have different levels of integrity. I have noted that over time, there are a couple of stones I used that are beginning to disintegrate as they have been exposed to the elements. Other stones are very stable and will probably remain unchanged for a thousand years. Get to know the nature of the stone you are working with and take it into account so that you don't end up with a crumbling structure.

Chapter 10

Preparing to Pour the Slab

It's now time to make the preparations to pour the slab that will sit on top of the containers to carry the weight of the dirt on top. Remember that the slab is intended to carry the weight of the dirt to the corner posts of the containers. The corner posts of the containers are designed to carry enormous amounts of weight which can be noted as you see many loaded containers stacked on the decks of container ships. Imagine the weight that the bottom container is carrying. We will not be requiring near that amount of weight as we bring the dirt back over the top of our containers.

Another function is to keep the dirt from pressing down on the roof of the containers and producing uneven divots. When you get your containers, as you walk along the roof, you will notice how it gives under your weight. We don't want this to happen under the weight of the dirt.

Obviously, the sheet metal of the roof is not the strength of the container.

In preparing to pour our slab, I am sure that I overbuilt, but I'd rather have too much than not enough. We elected to pour a 6 inch thick slab with rebar running both ways in a 12 inch on center grid pattern. This slab has been tested by the way, since there was a D4 Caterpillar driving all over it when it was packing and smoothing the dirt that we brought back over the top.

One of the things I wish we would have done to prepare for the slab would have been to have welded a steel plate about 4-6 inches wide the full length of the containers where they come together as well as down the front and side about 2 feet. We found that a small amount of water leaks through this crack down the center in the winter when there is a hydrostatic pressure produced that forces a small amount of water in under the slab. This really is a small amount of water, a few drips, and we have learned to cope with it to the point that we really don't notice it.

Another way of possibly addressing this problem might be to cover the slab and part way down the sides with a pond liner fabric. This could help shed the ground water away from the top of the container although there is an added cost.

One other thought I have had is that you could maybe extend the slab width out over the drain gravel on the sides so that any ground water getting onto the slab would be shed to the sides and down through the drain gravel.

Note the 12 " Steel grid pattern and the Poly Styrene forms on the side

Before you get too far in preparing the slab, I would suggest that you build a framing wall out of 2X4 and make that wall about ¼ inch higher than the container height. Make it long enough to run the whole length of the container. You can make it in sections for easier handling, but have it run the whole length. Once you have it built on the floor or on the ground outside, then place the top of it in the center of the container and use a sledge hammer or maul to tap the bottom into place until the wall is level. This should force the top of the container up that ¼ inch extra that you built into the wall. This will help to firm up the roof and keep it from sagging under the weight of the concrete as you pour it.

Another thing we learned is that it is wise to shut the doors and lock them into place before you pour so that the container shape doesn't get distorted under the weight of the newly poured concrete. We did not think to do that and our doors became very hard to close because the containers came slightly off square under the weight of the concrete. Just a thought for you to get better results.

Before you begin to place the steel grid, I would recommend that you cut any holes in the roof that you are going to place. This is the time to prepare for the solar tubes that you will want to have in place to get light down into the living area, especially in the back of the container where less light reaches from the front.

In preparing for our solar tubes, we measured the outside measurement of the down tubes that bring the light down into the living area. In our case we used tubes that were 12 inches in diameter. We decided that galvanized steel culvert would make a good outer tube that we could place the solar tube into so that the more fragile solar tube would not have contact with the earth. You could probably use a heavy plastic drain pipe if you could find one of sufficient diameter. We chose to use a 14 inch diameter culvert pipe so that we would have plenty of room to fit the solar tube inside.

We cut the culvert to a length sufficient to account for the slab thickness, the insulation on top of the slab and then the 3 feet of dirt to come over the top. By the way, we also had to buy extension tubes for the solar tubes since this distance was greater than the standard length that came with the routine setup.

As we installed the cut sections of culvert over the holes we cut in the container roof, we thought that using "Black Jack" roofing tar would be enough to seal out any water, especially as we were pouring the concrete around the culvert sections. This proved to not be satisfactory when we got into our first rainy season. When the soil got saturated, there was a slow drip around the circumference of the tube. I developed a circular catch channel that still let the light through to catch the drips as a solution to this issue but I think there might be a better way of installing these tubes.

One idea is that you could weld a bead around the steel tube and the roof. This would require a welder that knew how to weld galvanized steel with corten steel as this is what containers are made of. I'm not sure of the process, but talk to a local welder and get some input from them.

Another idea is to place the culvert in a bed of bitumen like what is used in a shower bed under the tile. It is possible that you may need to put some plastic around the outside of the bitumen to keep it in place while the concrete is poured into the slab area.

This is also the time to plan for anything else that needs to go through the roof such as stove pipe for a wood stove, vents for the bathroom and water heater, and possibly electric, gas, or water if you didn't bring them up through the floor. In our case, we had not brought these up through the floor so we used one of the 14 inch culverts to put all the services through plus a smaller solar tube in the bathroom area. So we have an 8 inch solar tube, a 5 inch water heater vent, a 3 inch fan vent, water pipe, gas pipe, and main electric wire; all coming through the culvert. They all fit and it has worked out well. I will show you how we prevent leaks in a later chapter.

Two more considerations are: an emergency exit and a whole-house air exchange. For the emergency exit we took a 55 gallon drum and cut a hole in the roof to accommodate as an emergency exit. This has proved to be very unsatisfactory, even though having an emergency exit is an excellent idea we think that it would have been better to use round cement sections built up from the slab to ground height, sealed both inside and outside to prevent water seepage and then an escape hatch constructed for the top that can only be opened from the inside of the container.

For the whole-house air exchange you will also need to cut a hole in the roof of a container. We made provision for this in the master bedroom with a 14" hole into which we put a fan that we can bring fresh air into the house or pull stale air out of the house by opening the front-of-container windows as little as 2" and turning on the fan.

Once all the holes are cut in the roof and the culverts are in place, (I would recommend you use smooth-sided culverts), you can begin to lay out the steel re-bar into the grid pattern. It is important for the steel not to lay directly onto the roof for the concrete pour so you should get some "dobbie blocks" to place under the steel periodically and keep it a couple of inches off the roof. It is also a good idea to wire the intersections of the steel so that they do not slip around once they are placed.

If you are going to pour the edge of the slab to come out past the walls (which I recommend you do) you will need to set up forms for the sides of the slab using 2X6 boards with stakes on the outside to keep the concrete from pushing the boards out.

At the front of the container, I used redwood 2X6's and screwed some long deck screws through them into the area that the concrete filled. These boards I wanted to stay in place after I took the forms away so I could use them in constructing the porch roof that I added on later.

Another preparation of the steel was to place steel coming up every 2 feet at the front of the container. This provided steel reinforcement tied into the slab at the front end of the container so that I could build a block wall right at the front of the container to push the dirt up against as we brought the dirt back over the top of the containers. I also filled these block with concrete so that it would be solid and strong.

Culverts coming up through the new concrete

NOTE: A suggestion for your consideration is that you put some kind of material, i.e. pond liner, around the culverts to protect them from the cement and the erosion action of the dirt. This will greatly enhance the longevity of the culverts.

Once your preparations are made for pouring the slab, it's time to get the concrete out to your site. I recommend that you also arrange to have a concrete pump available during the pour as well unless you have a lot of friends with wheelbarrows. It doesn't hurt to have several friends on site during the pour even with a pump.

The slab does not need to be finished off with a smooth finish. A rough trowel is just fine. Make sure and use a tamper to get the cement all settled into all the spaces. This also brings the "cream" to the top so it is easier to level everything off.

Using tampers to bring up the "cream" – also note the rebar coming up at the front that will connect the front block wall to the slab.

Chapter 11

Framing Walls and Partitions

Once the concrete has set up on the roof of the container, it's time to begin to frame in the walls and partitions for the final layout of your new home. Framing a container home is different from any other framing techniques I have ever been involved with. One of the things to consider is that you don't want to put any holes in the outer walls of the containers. These holes make primary targets for rust to begin and also are water magnets, so you need to come up with a different way to stabilize the walls.

There is a square metal bar at the top and bottom of the container that ties all the corners and makes up the main strength structure of the containers. All the roof and wall panels are welded to this bar. There is also a thick 1 ¼ inch mahogany plywood floor in the container. These two items are the main anchoring points to which you can attach screws and bolts to.

The other tool you have for anchoring your walls and partitions is friction. Let me explain. If you make the frame for your wall 1/8 inch longer than the actual measurement, you can use a sledge hammer or mall and force the wall into position and there is enough pressure on top and bottom plates to hold the wall into place by friction. Once in place, it is very difficult to move in any direction. We did this with most of our walls, but at the same time making sure they were all tied to each other, we don't have any free-standing walls.

It is better to screw all your joints together rather than using nails. The screws offer a more permanent and more solid connection and there is much less splitting of wood or moving the walls out of place with the hammering of nails. The screws work well to anchor all the floor plates to the plywood floors of the containers as well. You can also screw the walls together and they help hold each other in place. Actually the walls in our container are just as solid as any conventional walls I have ever worked with.

For the same reasons as using screws for the framing, you should also use screws for the sheet rock later on as you finish out the walls. You don't want to be doing a lot of hammering and risking moving the walls once in place.

Since we used the high cube (9 feet 6 inch) containers, we had a lot of extra room overhead so every place I put a closet, I also framed in a cupboard over the closet for additional storage. It is amazing how much storage this provided. Even in the kitchen, we were able to put in another row of cabinets for added storage. Since you have a relatively small footprint of floor space, all this extra storage is a real bonus.

Extra Storage Cupboard above closet

One of the things you are going to want to do is to cut through the adjoining walls in a couple of areas to open up the floor space and give your layout several areas that are 16 feet wide instead of just 8 feet. In order to make these cuts, I bought a metal cutting blade for my circular saw and I also bought a metal grinder that could do both grinding and cutting into sharper angles and spaces than the circular saw could handle. Be sure and wear protective goggles when performing this work because you do not want any metal fragments getting into your eyes – and there are many metal fragments flying around during this process. I also recommend that you use ear protection during this process since there is a lot of noise going on and you want to protect your hearing. I even used a mask so I wouldn't have to breathe the dust that the grinding produced.

Making a cut into the side to open up a room

Once you have made the cuts on one of the walls and removed that panel of the wall of the container, go to the other side, the other container, and measure very carefully so you are certain to make your cut exactly opposite of the first cut. Once you are sure of your marks, proceed to make the cut out of the second panel. If you have made your measurements and cuts carefully you should have an opening that looks like this:

Our first cut through – really opens it up!

In every place I cut out part of the wall, I made sure to place a wooden beam so that any support for the roof that I may have removed by taking that section of the steel wall out would be replaced by the beam. I designed it so that the beams would run up the side of each cut as pillars and then a lintel beam across the two pillars to support the weight from the roof. I also cut channels using a dado blade on my table saw on the side of the pillars and lintel that came in contact with the metal so that the metal would hide into the wood and there would be no sharp edges exposed.

The beams that I used were certainly larger than needed. I used 6X6 for the pillars and 6X10 for the lintel beam. I was able to get this lumbar at a Re-Store (Habitat for Humanity) outlet for pennies on the dollar of what you would normally pay at a retail outlet, so I figured there would be no problem with a little "over build".

Pretty Beefy Uh?

In the end, I cut 3 different places in the walls to open things up. A 7 ' cut opened up the living room in the front of the containers and another 7' cut opened up the master bedroom in the back of the containers. The other opening was a 3' cut to make a hallway that led to the two bedrooms from the bathroom.

Another helpful hint I discovered in making the layout for the partitions and then placing them was to use a felt tipped marker and draw the layout onto the floor once it was finalized. This helped to make the measurements as well as a point to bring the floor plates to before screwing them into place. It just seemed to make things come into place much better. Once the floor plates were screwed onto these markings, the rest of the wall could be leveled using a bubble level and then attached to each other for final positioning.

In framing out the end walls (just behind the container doors) I measured back from a closed door enough to account for the framing thickness plus sheetrock and finish on the inside plus siding and trim on the outside so that once the walls were completed and finished, you could still close the steel doors if you chose to do so. In order to make a nice tight fit and not have gaps to the outside, we also used spray in foam to seal up any cracks in these end walls.

In our home, we wanted to let in as much light as possible through the front, so we used large windows on one side of the container (two 3'X5' windows) and a 6 foot sliding glass door on the other side for the entrance. This gives a very nice open feeling for our living room/dining area space.

A view from our living room – into breakfast nook

I recommend that you use double pane glass for these because you want to maximize the insulation qualities of your dwelling and this front area will be where much of the heat loss in winter and cooling loss in summer can take place. This is also another reason why it is a good idea to use sealing foam on all the cracks so there are minimal air leaks and drafts.

Insulation is definitely recommended for these end walls, and we also insulated most of the other walls since it helps to cut down on the amount of sound that travels through. We found that when living in a smaller square footage area, it is more important to insulate against sound travel. You can make up your own mind on that issue.

We noticed in our home that the gravel that was filled into the sides of the containers tended to make the sides bulge in slightly. This is not a problem, except that it requires a little fudging when making the measurements for the walls that come up against these outer walls. We found that we had to frame to the measurement of the middle of the wall and then use trim to cover up the gaps on the top and bottom. Just another example of the flexibility required to work with this technique. A little trim covers a multitude of "fudges"!

Or if you are a really good carpenter you can custom fit your 2x4s to fit the bulges and indents perfectly, thereby eliminating the need for trim!

Chapter 12

Preparations for Bringing the Dirt Back Over the Top

Once the slab is poured, your excavation contractor is probably going to want to be finished as soon as possible so he can pull his equipment to another job. There are a couple of things that will need to be done before that can happen. First, the block wall on the top of the containers needs to be built. This will allow the dirt to be brought right to the edge of the container's roof without spilling on over.

We used 8X8X16 cement blocks to make this wall. We used rough on one side to give a more decorated look (in our opinion). Placing the block over the steel re-bar that we brought up from the slab, we built the wall 4 high of block or 32inches. This allowed for 8 inches of Poly Styrene insulation plus 2 feet of earth at the wall which sloped back to about 3 feet of earth at the back of the container. We then filled the block with concrete so that the wall would be very solid for the earth to come up against.

The next thing that needed to be done was to continue to bring the stone retaining wall on the sides out far enough to bring the dirt up to it and not spill around the sides. It is important to bring this retaining wall up high enough to meet the block wall and then slop down the sides until it meets the hillside.

Retaining wall to bring the dirt up to

Another are of preparation is placing the Poly Styrene insulation on the roof so it can be in place to be covered by the dirt. Since we were using 2 layers of the sheets, or 8" total, I took the extra precaution to stagger the sheets so there were not any gaps through both layers. I don't know if this really produced any appreciable effects but it made sense to me. As we got to the culverts for the solar tubes, we had to cut out areas for the sheets to fit over. I used a sheet rock saw to make these cuts. Poly Styrene board cuts very easy. I used my circular saw to make any straight cuts. There were a lot of Poly Styrene bubbles flying around during the cutting, but I guess one can have worse problems! NOTE: It probably would be a good idea to cover the Poly Styrene board with tar paper, just one more layer of protection between it and the dirt.

Using a Sheet Rock saw to cut out the Poly Styrene board.

Once all of these details have been covered, you can let the excavator come in and cover the top of the container. Make sure they are careful when bringing the dirt up to the retaining wall. Even though the walls are strong enough to hold back the dirt, a good push from a D4 could easily topple them. While they are covering with the dirt, make sure and get any large rocks out of the way so that they can smooth the dirt into a nice finish. Make sure the cat is driving back and forth packing the dirt as it is placed. A good finish will have the top almost level with the sides gradually sloping down to meet the natural contours of the hill side.

Chapter 13

Plumbing Considerations

Now that your walls are in place and your roof is covered with dirt, it's time to begin to provide for the niceties of life. In my estimation, plumbing is way down on the list of things I would rather be doing. In fact it might be dead last; but it has to be done if you want the "conveniences of civilization", so here we go.

One of the first things you need to do is to identify where your drains are going to go through the floor and tie into the plumbing drains that you have already placed in the ground under the containers. Remember when I advised you to carefully measure where you were going to place your drains and then measure from the back of the container to where the drain would be. Now is the time to identify that measurement and cut a hole into the floor where that drain will go. If you were careful in your measurements, you shouldn't be too far off. In my case, I was usually within a 6 inch radius of finding the drain in the ground.

Cut a rectangle of about 12 inches by 6 inches out to expose the area where you will try to find the drain. If you have a hard time getting the piece out, you can start a deck screw into it and then use the screw to pull the piece out. Save this piece as you may be able to use part of it to cover the remaining hole once the drain is through.

The next thing you will have to do is to scoop out the gravel that is covering the drain until you can identify the drain and clear enough area around it to glue your plumbing into it for the upright. You will probably have to do this by hand since there is usually not enough room to get any kind of tool in there. This sounds much easier than it actually is. The real problem that I ran into is that according to "Murphy's Law - what can go wrong will go wrong", and I might add, "Whatever can get in the way will get in the way".

Containers are made very strong by placing a channel beam every 11 inches across the bottom to mount the 1 ¼ inch Mahogany plywood on for a bomb proof floor. That's all fine and good until you want to get your drain to come up through the floor. You can bet donuts to dollars that every place your drain needs to come up is going to have one of these channel beams right smack dab in the middle! In the end, I usually had to cut the floor wider and then use the metal grinder to cut out a section of channel beam. In the end we got through it but my vocabulary was severely challenged.

Once you have identified and cleared the drain pipe in the ground, you will then glue up the appropriate angles and adapters to bring the upright up through the framed wall to the level at which you will connect your fixture. (This reminds me of a point I wish I would have thought about in my application. When you are putting the plumbing in the ground before the container is set into place, if that leg requires a "P-trap", put it in place while you have the luxury of digging the area with a shovel instead of a table spoon!) Then you will connect the stub out through the wall ready for the finish wall treatment to be applied (usually sheet rock).

Repeat this procedure for all the drains you have planned, until you have them all identified and stubbed out. By the way, write me and let me know if you ever find a drain that comes straight up with nothing in the way. You would be the first and I would like to buy you a cup of coffee!

As far as vents go, I made plans and brought vents up through the roof, but I since then I found out that there is a really neat gadget that removes the need for all that bother. It is a pipeless vent that has a one way valve on it that will keep the system covered unless there is a pressure buildup – I believe it is called a short-stack vent. I have used several now and have never had any problem with smells or drainage.

By practice, I have always been used to using copper pipe for my hot water supplies, but I know there are several other options out there so use what you are used to or have the equipment for. The cold side I just use schedule 40 PVC and glue it into place. One of the long runs I had to make to the kitchen sink I didn't have any wall to put the pipe into so I laid it along the floor right against the wall and then notched the cabinets on that back corner when I placed them hiding the pipes quite well. I wrapped the hot water supply with some insulating tape so that it would keep from affecting the cold water supply.

The rest of the plumbing will fit fairly routinely (as routine as plumbing gets!) within the rest of the wall framing. Since I brought the gas in through the roof, I used the corner bar to screw brackets in place to hold the gas pipe firm.

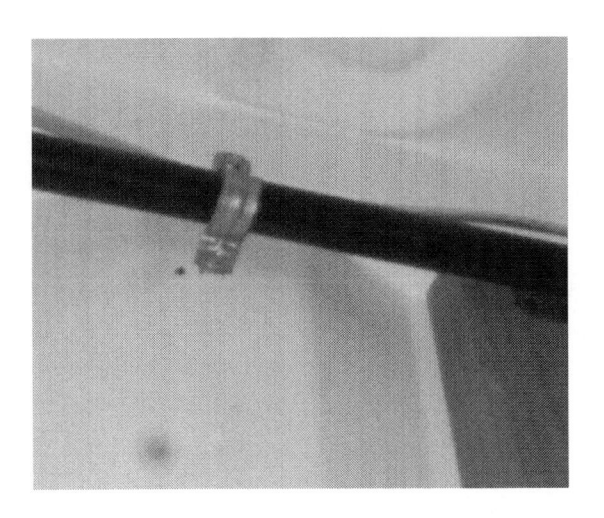

Detail of gas pipe bracketed to top of wall beam

This brings me to another consideration. Is it better to bring the water, gas and electric in through the floor or the roof? I will tell you my thoughts and why I did it the way I did. Once the containers are in place and the slab is on top along with the dirt, it is going to be next to impossible to make any changes in any of these applications. If you bring the services in through the roof, any change you need to make down the line such as remodeling will be much easier at least for these services. The sewer would still be a major issue, but these others would go much easier from the top.

There are advantages to coming up through the floor too, so you have to decide what you want to live with.

The water heater was installed in a closet behind the bathroom. Our design was to have the one culvert tube opening into the bathroom carry the water, gas and electric into the container and the vent for the water heater and room vent fan up and out the same culvert. There was also enough room to put a smaller 8 inch solar tube for light into the bathroom. With all of these in close proximity, we designed a closet on the back of the bathroom to put the electric panel and the water heater in as well as attach the main pipe for water supply. From this closet then runs all the services through the framed walls.

We used an instant hot water heater and since we are off grid, we ordered one that does not even need electricity to ignite. This one has a little water wheel that produces a small electric current that lights the flame when you turn the hot water tap on – pretty cool! The real fun part was getting the right angle on the vent to run from the water heater through the framing and then turn at the right angle to go up through the culvert. In the end it worked – amazing.

There are several reasons I recommend this type of water heater. The first is that it is so much smaller than a standard water heater so it takes up much less room that is so precious in this smaller footprint home. The unit is about 20" by 30" and comes out from the wall about 6". It is light and is hung on 2 screws mounted into a 2 X 4; once you have the pipes and vents hooked up, it just sits there with no issues like earthquake straps to bother with.

Another benefit is that the water is heated instantly, so that you are not ever running out of hot water. This means you can take a really long shower if you want to! The standard water heaters have a tank that the hot water is stored into and it kept hot by the fire coming on periodically to keep it hot. This means when you are using the hot water, you can run out when the tank empties, and it also means that you are using extra energy to keep the water hot continually.

These water heaters are a little more expensive than a standard water heater, but in my opinion, they are well worth the extra cost. I believe they recover that extra cost in a short time with the energy savings they offer. I even installed one in our conventional home years ago and enjoyed its benefits there too.

One thing I did discover was that you need good water pressure to make the hot water circuit come on. Since we are on gravity water pressure at our place, we couldn't get the hot water to kick in. After several frustrations, I finally determined that there wasn't enough water pressure.

My fix for that was to place a small 12 Volt RV water pump in line to the water heater so that when we turned the hot water on, it would turn on and increase the water pressure to around 45 psi. This was plenty of pressure to turn the hot water heater on and solved our issue. Living off grid requires lots of solutions like this that are unique to your setting. You have to think on your feet – but it's worth the effort!

Chapter 14

Electrical Considerations

When it comes to electrical, most of it goes the same as in any conventional structure. There are a few exceptions and we will cover these. In the first place, I do think I would bring my electric in under the container in my next installation. Use a good underground rated wire and bring it in its own ditch just like you did with the drains. Buried wire is quite reliable by experience, so underground should be fine. This gives you one less hole to seal up on the roof top.

I think I would still put the panel in the closet behind the bathroom. This gives it a nice fairly central location to run all the circuits from and keeps it out of the way. We found that a small panel (50 Amp) works fine since we are on solar and therefore use much less electricity than a standard household on the grid would use. We have never tripped a breaker yet.

In our case, we have our solar panels on our well pump house. The batteries and inverter are there as well; Our electric supply is 120 V that comes from the inverter.

I chose to have all my 12V electrical from the photovoltaic panels going into the batteries very closely installed. The lower the voltage, the bigger the wire you need to carry that voltage. By keeping all the 12V circuits close together, I didn't have to spend so much money on large diameter wire to carry the current very far. By inverting at the pump house close to the batteries, I am able to invert 12 V to 120 V and then carry the 120 V on a #12 wire up to the container about 300 feet away. Since it is a higher voltage, there is very little voltage drop. I measured the voltage at the container and it is still 117V.

This is what I elected to do because I am also pumping water with solar power, so I wanted my panels to be available for the pump as well. Besides, the roof of the pump house is an excellent place to mount the panels on our property. There are other ways of doing it specific to whatever piece of property you may be on; you just need to decide what is going to work well for you.

I know some people off grid who work with all 12V wiring and use 12V appliances and lighting fixtures. I know others who have a place for both 12V and 120V wiring in their homes so they can have either available. Like I said, there are many ways to work it.

Another reason that I chose to bring 120 V into the house was that I didn't want to spend all the extra money that is required to buy 12 V fixtures and appliances. For example, I checked out the price on a 12V refrigerator. It was nearly $2000 and it was a small one at that. Small is good when you're off grid, but I was able to find the same size refrigerator at the local big box building supplier for less than $200. That's a 10 to 1 difference and the 120V refrigerator has been running fine for years. My wife thinks next time we should invest in an LPG refrigerator. Some friends have one and they say the propane usage is about 1 ½ gallons per week. For our solar system we have to turn off the refrigerator at night (which is really hard on things in the freezer), to keep from using up the battery bank so as not to wake up to a dark house in the morning and the need to immediately start the generator for power. (We need more panels!) These same friends, who are also totally off grid, even have a dishwasher – my wife was really impressed with that detail. Next time I have a feeling there will be some extras added into the blueprints!

Since we are on solar and off grid, we have learned to do things a little differently, like I just said instead of letting your refrigerator run all the time, we keep a gallon of water frozen in the freezer compartment and then turn the refrigerator off during the night while it is not being opened and closed all the time. Everything stays fairly well and you do not use so much of your precious electricity. You actually learn lots of tricks that help you conserve the amount of power you use. We will talk more about that later.

Another benefit of bringing 120 V electricity to the home is that you can do all your wiring with standard supplies obtainable at any local building supplier. This saves a lot of money and time as well as frayed nerves from trying to find specialized suppliers for 12V equipment. It also makes it easier since you can use standard installation techniques to run your circuits. Electricity is one of my lesser skill sets, so this is where I obtained the expertise of a friend that was able to trouble shoot my mistakes and get our home functioning properly.

I mentioned that our electric panel is installed in a small utility closet behind our bathroom. The exact location may vary in your layout, but I recommend establishing such a small closet so that you can place all the main utility supplies within it and keep it central. This closet should contain the hot water heater, water supply shut-off, electric panel, and gas supply shut-off. The closet in our set up is close to the bathroom because this makes these utilities readily available without having to run too much length in bringing these utilities out to their respective locations.

As you run your electric lines out from the panel, there may be some places that do not have framed walls to do the normal technique for running wire. We found that you could run the wire either along the floor and tack it with a small plastic coated loop screwed into the square metal frame beam along the top as well as along the bottom— either way it works for where your run is going. The stores have coverings for these wires if you want a more finished look.

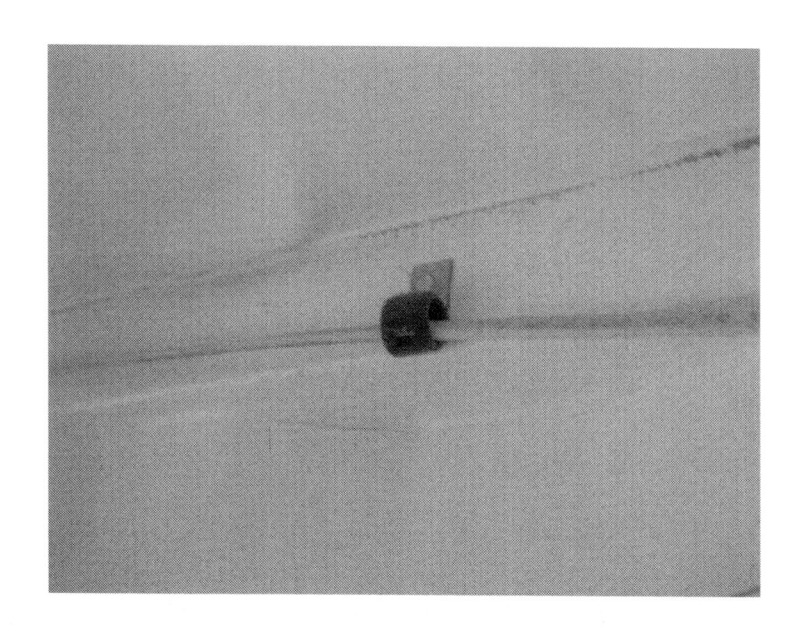

Detail of wire hanger screwed into corner beam

I elected to not drill or screw into the walls of the containers since I did not want to make openings through any metal parts that would be exposed to moisture. I felt that this could possibly encourage rust to get started by exposing bare metal from the drill sites. I'm not sure if this would actually be a problem since we placed the 18" of drain gravel all around the outside, but I just wanted to be careful. Once rust does get started, it becomes a real threat to your integrity.

In places where you need to put a receptacle that are not framed in, you can use surface mount boxes that are available at hardware stores. There is also available exposed wire coverings that fit to these surface mount boxes. I was able to find these in several different hardware suppliers. You can also use plastic capped staples to run the wire along any wood surface and keep it tidy looking. The key is to be adaptable and not afraid to try some new techniques or keep an eye out for new supplies.

I am always looking around in the big hardware stores for different ways of doing things. I know wives can be tempted to think we are just wasting time, but we are really "researching" so that we can come up with solutions. I encourage you to keep alert to the new supplies and techniques continuing that come to the market regularly.

Chapter 15

Cabinets and Cabinet Walls

The walls that you want to hang cabinets on must be treated differently if they are not framed walls. The sides of containers are wavy and the indent of each wave is about the thickness of a 2 x 4 but narrower. You can trim a 2 x 4 down to the width of the wave and then fix it in place by screwing in a small "L" bracket at the top and bottom into the square metal beams at the top and bottom of the walls. Wood screw the 2 x 4 into these "L" brackets at the top and bottom.

Detail on L-bracket placement

You now have a strong support on which to hang sheet rock and then hang the cabinets. These 2 x 4's end up being about 11" on center. Install one into every wave for the whole length of the cabinet wall so that you have plenty of wood to mount your cabinets.

SheetroSheetrock applied to 2X4's

In the picture above, you can see how the 2X4's are inserted into the wave of the container side. The sheet rock is held back so you can see the construction technique, but you can fill the space up to complete the wall coverage. This actually makes a very sturdy structure for placing cabinets. Outside of the slightly different spacing from the standard 16"on center, installation of the cabinets is fairly standard.

As far as the framed walls, I still recommend that you use screws instead of nails. Nailing will work the walls and possibly move them out of place. Nails also work loose over time. I much prefer the sheet rock screws, they hold better and do not seem to loosen over time. I also think they are easier to install.

Any other finishing of the walls is mostly standard to regular techniques for plastering. One slight difference is that the outer walls have a slight bow as a result of the pressure of the gravel from the outside, so you may want to apply a small piece of trim to hide this small gap. It comes down to your preference.

Our Kitchen with Cabinets Installed

Once your walls are prepared, you can cover them with anything from paint to paneling to fabric. One of the options that you have with a steel walled container is that you can even decorate with magnetic accessories. We kept some of the walls with the basic steel of the containers but used a thin fabric to add an interesting effect. See picture below.

This is our Living Room

Another option you have for wall treatment is the metal loops that are welded every 4 feet on both floor and ceiling. These can be removed or kept in place for fastening cables, wires or ropes to and installing unique wall treatments. I used one to hang a speaker from for our stereo so that I could preserve precious floor space. We also have several of our pictures and tapestries hanging from them.

The only limit is your imagination. You can cut them out, but don't do it too soon. Make sure you really want them gone, first before you cut.

Chapter 16

Flooring

The flooring issue is actually one of the easier aspects of interior decorating in the container. Since the floor of containers is made of 1 ¼ inch thick mahogany plywood, it is very sturdy. If the floors were not so gouged by the endless forklifts and pallets scraping against them, they could be sanded and varnished, but sadly this is not the case. In order to get a nice floor finish, you will most likely have to apply some sort of standard covering. We used vinyl flooring in the kitchen and bathroom, and a couple of rooms have laminated interlocking flooring.

Interlocking Laminated Flooring Being Installed

We also used large area rugs in the living room. You could install wall to wall carpeting as well but you will have a small metal strip on each edge of the container that will show. There is a metal section of flooring at the back of each container, about 4 feet in from the end wall and it stretches from side to side. We covered this with carpets as it is our master bedroom, but It would also be easy to install wood flooring, tile, or any other standard floor treatment.

I have also noticed some great epoxy type floor coverings that are used in garages and industrial applications that really don't look too bad and are very durable.

Speaking of Epoxy, I'm sure if you wanted a quaint look but easy care, you could find a clear leveling type coat that would allow the wood to show through but have an even surface. That would allow the character of all the gouges to be preserved in an interesting array.

There is also an issue of how to cover the area where the containers come together and the wall has been cut out to expand the room. In our case, we ground the metal down as far as we could to remove any sharp edges and then we placed carpet pieces over them to keep the area from showing and give it softness in case someone steps on that area, but I do recommend that you go to a door shop and get a custom threshold to fit over this area. It could be either wood or metal. A custom woodshop may also have some good suggestions. The threshold space is to wide and too high for a standard door threshold. Once again, be inventive. There are many solutions just waiting to be found.

Chapter 17

A Porch Roof

The need to build a porch roof was not as evident when we first installed the containers as It later became after we had spent some time living in the containers. Just one rainy winter and hot, southern exposure summer convinced us that a porch roof would be a great addition.

It is a good idea for winter because it provides a protected area for entering and exiting on rainy days. It also gives a good place to store some things that you want to keep out of the weather like outdoor chairs and barbeques. The proper angle of the roof slope will also allow the passive solar heat exchange from the lower angle of the sun in the southern sky, and if you so choose the porch roof is another good location to put more solar panels, especially if the roof has a southerly exposure which ours does.

It is a good idea for the summer as well. When the hot summer sun is beating down, it is a great thermal cushion to keep the inside cooler since there is shade in front of the door and windows. Once again, the correct angle on the roof slope will provide this shade from the higher angle of the summer sun. Now that we have built this roof, we have really come to appreciate its protection both summer and winter.

We built the porch roof by pouring concrete pads with brackets for attaching 4X4's to attach the roof structure. The ridge of the roof was designed to set on the block wall that we built on top of the slab to hold the dirt back. We just made a short 18" back side of the roof from the ridge to the ground so that it would shed the water off the ridge to the back of the block wall. We gave it a 4/12 pitch and brought it out 8 feet from the containers. This was enough to give the protection we desired, but at the same time, let the sun shine in during the winter.

Our Porch Roof serves very nicely

One of the things we discovered was that there is a OSB sheathing for roofing that has foil, called a radiant barrier, on the down side, and it is amazing how much heat this reflects away during the summer months. You can use what you want, this is just a suggestion. The same goes for the shingles or shakes or whatever you want to finish with. I used standard framing technique and design for the construction, from framing to finish.

As I have stated before another benefit of having this large flat surface connected to your home is that it is an excellent place to mount solar panels for your electricity.

Even though we have most of our panels on our pump house, we have now added a backup system installed on this roof so it has effectively given us more options. It is always good to have areas for expanding your systems as the need arises.

Chapter 18

Ventilation

In building an underground home, great care needs to be taken to provide adequate ventilation so that the air remains fresh throughout the home. This is important for all seasons, but especially in the winter when there is more moisture. It is very important that there not be too much moisture build-up in the container. Moisture leads to starting rust, and you don't want rust to get started.

In our case, we installed one of the culvert tubes just to be used for air exchange. These are the same tubes that we used for the solar light tubes I described earlier. We actually installed the ventilation tube very close to one of the solar tubes. We have a fan set up to pull air from the home into the vent which then pulls the air from the front rooms and eventually from the door and front windows.

In the winter, we try and exchange the air when the sun is shining in under the porch roof so that we are bringing in warm air. Using a small catalytic heater during rainy days also helps keep the air dryer during the winter.

During the summer, we exchange the air during the cooler evening and night times. This allows and helps to keep the temperature cooler by several degrees during the hotter parts of the day as well. Sometimes, if it has been very hot during the day, we will place a fan in front of the door to blow cooler air in as the evening advances. This helps in the immediate interval as well as accomplishes the vital air exchange.

In talking with people who live in more humid environments, I believe that it is important to suggest that one consider using a de-humidifier in such a climate. Our California climate has not warranted this so I did not think it necessary to install one, but areas like the South-East of the US would certainly need to consider using a de-humidifier. Once again, the more moisture you can keep out of your home, the better it is for the longevity of the structure.

I have also seen various electrical systems for preventing rust advertised. These are very similar to what the Navy uses to keep rust from destroying their ships from contact with the salt water. They use electrodes applied to the metal that is connected to a low voltage current that effectively "sacrifices the electrode before allowing rust to start in on the metal they are protecting. A little research on the internet should reveal several sources to supply this type of system should you have a wet environment to combat.

Another consideration you may want to address is whether or not to install a filter with your ventilation. We did not do so, but I have talked with people who have done so. There are various levels of filters to consider as well. The first level would be just to filter out particulate matter from the air. This would be the most basic level, and least expensive.

The next level would be at the HEPA level which would be a benefit to those who suffer from allergies. This level of filtration becomes more difficult to maintain and much more expensive.

The final level that I will address would be a filter that could filter out biological warfare agents, and nuclear fallout particles. There are such filter systems available, but once again, they are very expensive and require much more careful architecture to support their proper installation and use. In areas of Israel where chemical warfare is a real threat, these types of filters are being installed successfully.

If your reason for building is to construct a hardened bunker type facility, then you may well decide to go with the third option. However, since we were building a home in the country to enjoy the benefits of geothermal heating and cooling, we decided to once again keep it simple. The choice once again is yours. I'm just trying to get you to think about the different considerations ahead of time so you are prepared at the level you choose.

When designing whatever level of system, you will need to decide how fast you want to be able to do an air exchange, and then install a fan that can move the sufficient volume of cubic air in the period of time you desire. Fans are usually rated in cubic feet per minute, so make sure you have it properly sized.

One thing I would suggest is that you acquire a simple Radon detection device and keep your Radon levels monitored periodically. Radon is a naturally occurring gas that seeps up from the ground in certain areas of the country. It is odorless and tasteless, but can have serious health consequences for some individuals.

Chapter 19

Wood Stoves and Heating

We have found that we do not need much additional heating for our home. During the very cold days of winter, the temperature remains around 63 degrees Farenheit and that is usually comfortable enough for us if we are moving around. We do have a RV catalytic heater that runs on propane that we turn on first thing in the morning to warm up the house and after the sun goes down to help keep the house warm on those cold days when the passive solar just isn't enough. And sometimes we turn on the heater when we want to snuggle up and read a book or work on the computer or just want to be a bit warmer than 63 degrees!.

The heater runs on propane so I plumbed in a line that comes off the back of the cooking stove and through the kitchen wall into the living room. This has a quick connect fitting on it so we can take the heater out of the way in the warmer months of the year. As I mentioned before, we have brought the propane gas line in through the roof. It is not quite perfect as we have brought the pipe down the wall to the back of the stove, but with a little creativity, we were able to bring the sheet rock up to both sides of the pipe and paint the pipe so it doesn't look too out of place. I do think next time I would bring the gas line in from underneath the container instead of through a roof vent.

Another possibility for heating would be a wood stove. This could easily be done either of two ways. My first suggestion is to dedicate a culvert tube to accommodate the triple-wall chimney sections of the wood stove. I would put the wood heater in the living room, and position the culvert section appropriately to where you want the wood stove to be placed. Make sure you have this culvert correctly placed and the hole cut before the cement is poured and the dirt is covered back onto the container roofs.

A second way to deal with running the chimney outside could also be to bring it out the front wall. This would place your wood stove on the front wall, and would take room from the dining area, in our case, but it is going to take room no matter where you put it. One good thing is that you have metal wall backing it up if you put it with the chimney going up through the roof. Fire proofing would not be an issue, but you might want to use some special paint or have a heat shield in place to keep the paint from peeling with the heat.

The size of stove you would install would need to be quite small. These containers hold a lot of heat and a larger stove would run you out of the house. I have seen some nice small sized wood stoves that would work well for this application. Even a small sized stove still has enough surface area to place cooking kettles on, which is another benefit to having a wood stove.

I am in favor of the catalytic heater because it uses so little space and you do not have to worry about peeling any paint, or making any preparations to avoid such. It has worked fine for us. The only disadvantage is that if we were to come into a time when propane were no longer available, then a wood stove would really be the answer. In our case, I would just remove the solar light from the living room culvert tube, and place the wood stove chimney through that, and keep on going. Always have a backup plan!

In talking about solar energy, I believe that you could also develop a system of heating water in the day time through coiled black irrigation pipe and storing that warm water in a tank, then circulating that warm water through a radiant floor system when the heat is needed. This would take a lot more engineering, but I have seen these systems and they are pretty neat! This would also have an added cost involved, but if you had the bucks and wanted to be totally dependent on solar, you might consider it.

One last thing to mention in this department; If you were to use really good insulated curtains for the front windows and door, as well as devise an insulation to place in the solar tubes, especially at night, I believe this would make another several degrees difference in how warm it would stay in the containers even without heating them. So far we have not done this since we are happy with how things are, but if you are in a colder winter climate, this could well be worth considering.

Chapter 20

Off Grid Considerations

There are several things one needs to consider when deciding to live "Off Grid". There are also several different levels of "Off Grid" to consider. When I use the term, I mean that we are not hooked up to the electric utilities, public water source, sewer, gas, or phone service. We do not have garbage service, nor do we even have the county available to grade our road, although the gravel road that our road comes off of is graded a couple times a year.

The power poles do come within 700 feet of our property, but when we inquired on getting power out to our place, we were given an estimate of close to $20,000 which was a bit daunting for us as we were paying as we go. At that time, we decided to take that same money and invest in installing solar equipment that would not have a monthly bill attached to it. 10 years later, we are extremely glad that we made that choice. We haven't had a utility bill for those

10 years and when the grid goes down during a storm, it's not a problem for us.

To be honest, not being hooked up to the electric does have its challenges. There are some things we just cannot run because it would require too much of our precious electricity. We have become very careful of what we leave on and even small lights and things that bleed out electricity over time. We do have a generator backup so that at times when we need an extra boost, we can start it up; like when we need to iron some clothes. You have to design your system so that you have the right amount of battery storage, solar panels, and inverter capacity to handle the loads you will require.

There are many books available about designing a solar system. I have read quite a few. I will not presume to write another one; just start reading and asking questions and researching on the internet. I started with a small system and kept adding to that. It has been a steep learning curve but it has had its rewards. As I write this chapter, the price on solar equipment, especially the solar panels is the lowest it has ever been. It is a very good time to be thinking about installing a solar system. Panels are coming close to $1 per watt, which would have been unimaginable only 5 years ago.

Another area of being off grid is phone service. We are in an area that is minimal coverage from a major cell provider. We have tried different services and there seems to be little difference between the competitors. We also use a cell device for our computer service which ends up being slow, but at least we have something. You might want to consider this when buying your property. If communication is important to you, you might want to make sure you have a decent signal on the land you are looking at.

Of course this is one of the aspects of "Off Grid" that is debatable. Some demand that if you are going to be off grid, you will not have communications capacity. Some people hike into their homestead and leave everything behind. We have not gone that far yet. I am just bringing up the cell phone idea to think about, as you decide what level of off grid you want to participate in.

There are various levels of services we can set up in our area. We could install a large propane tank and have a delivery truck bring the gas out to us, but we have elected to use smaller portable (90#) tanks and transport them into town to get filled when we need them. We could also set up a garbage pick-up, but we elect to do that ourselves as well.

In rural areas, it is better to have a well than to depend on a municipal supply for water. Our well is very good with a never ending supply of pure sweet-tasting cold water. We pump it by solar up to tanks at the top of our property and then gravity feed it through our irrigation and home supply system. If anything goes wrong with the system, I have to fix it. I can't call the water company because I am the water company, so I keep extra supplies around in case I get a break or a valve fails. Our well is a real blessing. I will tell you more about the water system and design in the next chapter.

All of these systems that you install on your land/homestead will become the core of how you provide for the essentials and comforts that you decide you want to have available for your life style. Once these systems are in place, as you keep them maintained, they will provide you with the "utilities" that you will connect your home to. The main thing you need to remember is to know how your systems work so that when something goes wrong, you are the repair person that you depend on to get it up and running again. You want to know your systems so that you are not dependent on someone else to fix them when something goes wrong. You will want to have extra parts on hand and not have to run into town every time something goes wrong. This is part of being off grid – to be self-sufficient. When everyone else is waiting 5 days for the utility company to restore power, you can be comfortably enjoying your life with no worries. It's a whole new way of thinking and living!

Chapter 21

Well and Water System

If you are going to be truly off grid, you will have to work out how you are going to supply water to your property. In our area, wells are the usual method although some have not been successful in hitting a water source and are confined to hauling water in tanks from a municipal source. Many wells in our area are 2-3 gallons a minute which is barely able to support a household, but by using storage tanks and pumping 24 hours a day at a slow rate, one can manage.

In our case, I talked with a local geologist and found out where the most likely place to find water would be. We also had some prayer partners who joined us in asking our Heavenly Father where He thought the well should be. On the basis of that information, we contacted a drilling company and arranged for them to come and start drilling the site. My wife was so confident she had heard specifically from the Lord that the well would be at 220 feet and that the water would be abundant and pure and clean that she wrote that in a note that she sent along with the key to our gate so they could get started when we weren't there.

As the well got started, they got into the bedrock and got to a place where the bit angled too much and they couldn't re-engage it so they had to pull out and start a new site some 20 feet away from the original site. As they drilled, they got to 160 feet and had not gotten more than 2 gallons a minute. They told us they had just drilled through 1000 feet of bedrock at a previous site and had only got a 1-2 gallon per minute flow; they were asking if we wanted to go any further because they said that once you hit bedrock, there was probably no water below it.

We were confident in the word that my wife had received from the Lord, that we told them to go ahead and keep drilling, and that we would reassess when we got to 220 feet. My wife was going to town with another friend to get some supplies and she had quite a talk with her Heavenly Father on the way into town. She reminded Him that He had promised a good well, but things weren't looking so good. In the meantime, I and our friend's husband had stayed behind to work on the foundation of our barn, getting it prepped for a cement pour the next day.

As we were working we suddenly heard the sound of the drilling rig change and when I looked down where it was, I could see water pouring out from all over, even the top of the rig. We went running down to see what had happened. The fellow drilling was quite excited and told us he had just broken into a major water source. Just then my wife and friend came back from town and hearing the commotion coming up from the well drilling site came running down to see what was happening. When she heard we had struck water, she immediately asked how deep the drill was. It was at exactly 220 feet. By the time all the drilling was complete and the pump was set, the driller told us he could only measure up to 60 gallons a minute and it was way over that. The water actually pushes back up to within 40 feet of the surface, even today. I think you could call that abundant! People still drive to our place to fill jugs with drinking water because it has a very good sweet taste too.

Once the well was established, the next task was to begin to lay out the water lines for irrigation and domestic use. I decided to install a system that would operate on gravity since we were on a hillside. The difference in elevation from the well to the top of our property is almost 100 feet. This gives ample opportunity to develop sufficient water pressure just from the gravity. 100 feet of elevation will produce 45 psi of pressure. Even at the level of our orchard, we still produce about 18 psi which is enough to operate a low pressure drip irrigation system. There are many irrigation systems that require you to lower the pressure for them to work properly, so this is the type we used. If you visit any irrigation supplier, they will show you several options.

Irrigation is a big consideration because we wanted to be able to grow our food on our property. This to us was one of the reasons we were going off grid. If you are disconnecting from the grid for your utilities, it would also be a good thing if you could grow all the food you needed instead of having to depend on the grocery distribution system. Anything you can figure out to do on your own property gets you closer to being self-sufficient.

To be honest with you, if I had it to do over, I would change the way we laid out the agriculture production. We have good gardens and the orchard is doing fairly well, but I have since discovered a much better way of doing things that costs less and is much more efficient. I will spend a chapter sharing this concept with you. Agriculture is a vital aspect of developing a property for off grid as far as I am concerned, and irrigation is the key to successful agriculture.

I will give you a suggestion here. I bought an old backhoe tractor and did all my own ditches with it. When I was finished, I sold the tractor for what I paid for it and had all the hundreds of hours of work done by it for virtually free. If you don't know how to run one, learn. It could save you a lot of money and they are so handy to have around when you are in the building phase.

I ran a 1- 1/4 " line from the well up to a 2500 gallon tank that I set at the top of our property. This enabled us to fill the tank from the well. I have found out that a well pump lasts much longer if you run it for long periods of time instead of on and off frequently keeping a pressure tank up to pressure. It takes our tank about 2 hours to fill, so that is really good on our pump. Since we changed over to a solar pump, it is slower to fill a tank, about 5 hours. In the summer, when we need more water for irrigation, we usually have to pump another tank in the evening by generator to keep enough water for all our needs, especially with the orchard.

The pipe down from the tank starts out at 1-1/4" to the main divisions. At these divisions, I continued the lines using 1" schedule 40 PVC. When I split off to supply hydrants and taps, I dropped the size to ¾" and placed ¾" faucets and valves on them. Once the supply was into the home and other structures, the wall plumbing was done in ½" pipe which is standard for household plumbing.

The reason for diminishing the diameter of the pipe with each branch off is to help maintain the pressure at optimal levels throughout the system and be able to use more than one tap at a time while still having adequate pressure and flow rates. You can get really technical and calculate the diameters and flow rates but I found that the system I just described to you works quite well. Once again, an irrigation supplier can help you with planning a good layout.

Another consideration in our area is wildfire danger through the summer months. I have added ¾" risers on both the fill line coming up to the tank as well as the gravity line coming down from the tank. These are evenly spaced along the perimeter of our land so that if a fire does occur, we have options for getting as much water as possible to keep the fire down. Another recommendation is to find out what fitting the local fire department uses and have one of those fittings available so that a tanker can fill from your tank if necessary.

As you lay out and install your irrigation/water supply system, make sure you keep an updated accurate map of how the pipes are laid out. It is important for future times when you need to do repairs or install new lines, or even place new structures. If you know where not to dig, or at least be very careful as you dig, you can save yourself a lot of trouble.

Chapter 22

Agriculture

As I have mentioned already, the ability to grow the food you eat is very important for becoming off grid. We had this in mind when we purchased our 10 acres. We thought that would be enough to sustain ourselves with what we could grow. We started out by taking an organic orcharding class and learned how to amend the soil so that it would provide optimal nutrients for the fruit trees we wanted to plant.

We also marked out our garden areas and began to supplement those and get them ready for planting. It took a lot of work, money and time to get the soil into shape to begin to produce the crops we were anticipating. As we launched into our first garden planting and began trying to keep our orchard alive through the first of the summer heat, we began to realize some things we had not thought of.

First, we had and still have, a real problem with varmints, especially gophers. They have been responsible for taking out some or our orchard trees and many of our garden plants. They have also done a number on our irrigation system and shunted water where it was not supposed to go and kept it from where it should go. Even with our soil work that we have done, there is still need for more organic material to be added to help conserve water from evaporating too fast.

Here's what I would do differently and am in the planning stages of converting over to. I have been studying a system called Aqua-ponics developed by a fellow down in Australia. The main idea is that you have growing beds that are elevated off the ground and use gravel or clay pellets for the growing media. There are also tanks of fish associated with the growing beds. As the fish poop in the tanks, the water is circulated into the grow beds and the plants use the nitrates from the fish as their fertilizer. The plants also adjust the pH of the water back to where it is compatible with the fish, and the process starts all over again. This is a complete Nitrogen cycle that gives you both organic vegetables and fish for a protein source in your diet.

Aquaponic System I made in Thailand

The plants grow about twice as fast, and they produce about twice as much fruit so there is a 4 fold increase in production. Then you have the fish that can be grown very dense because the plants are keeping the pH optimal so the fish are getting to market size in about 6 months. You don't even have to have level land to operate on, and you can use green houses to operate year round. You can also use solar to power the pumps that you will need. And you won't have any gopher problems.

The cost of setting this system up is very reasonable and if I had known about it when we started building our soil, I would have put the money into this system and been up and running by now. It uses much less water as well, only needing enough to replace for evaporation.

The system can also grow fruit trees and they do much better and grow much quicker because they are under optimal conditions for water and nutrients constantly. There is virtually nothing that you cannot grow with this system. You can even use solar coils of black plastic irrigation pipe to regulate the water temperature so the fish remain productive throughout the year, even in cold snaps.

You can get more information by going to:

http://www.aquaponics.net.au/

http://www.youtube.com/watch?v=bCV7DABEz20

This is some of the evidence that it works

It is my opinion this technique of agriculture/aquaculture is the most promising that I am aware of. I believe that it has much promise for the future. There is a major project being conducted at the University of Wisconsin on a large commercial scale, and I'm sure more information will be forthcoming.

Obviously, there are other successful technologies out there being used and developed, so I won't say this is the only way, it's just a very good way. I just encourage you to do some research and spend some time investigating and asking questions so you can put together a successful system that will feed you and possibly become a good income source.

A fruitful agricultural program is vital to the success of a truly self-sustaining off-the-grid homestead. Careful research and preparation will be time well spent.

Chapter 23

Final Thoughts

I hope that I have given you some food for thought. It has been amazing to me to see the interest that our home has generated. Many people tell me they have thought about the idea of building this way but just didn't know where to start. I have had many people drive up to our place and start taking pictures and asking questions because they had always wanted to see a place built like this.

The previous chapters have been written in an effort to explain the steps and details of building in this style. It is virtually impossible to give every detail and cover every aspect of the process, but I believe that I have included enough to enable you to build a successful project. Many of the finer details become evident as you go through the process. A moderate degree of "thinking things through" will be required on your part. Sometimes you may have to take a friend out to dinner or trade a favor to get some of the knowledge and experience that you will need to complete this project. I understand that there are various levels of experience and skill that each of you will bring to a project like this, but I also believe that the desire to make this happen will overcome many deficits you may have on your part.

Do not be afraid to ask questions. That is where most of my knowledge and skill base come from – just asking questions, reading instructions, and watching an expert do their work. Now-a- days, there are many Youtubes available that demonstrate an almost endless variety of skills and knowledge bases.

I have said all that to say this – Just do it – get in there and start – don't worry about what you don't know. There are many resources available to you, and if you want it bad enough, it will become your reality. Build it, it may not be perfect, but it will be comfortable and adequate and you will have the satisfaction of doing it yourself and enjoying the fruits of your labor.

I also offer my knowledge and experience, should you need it. I will be available by e-mail should you have any questions. You may reach me at:

waterfallofgrace@hotmail.com

It has been a joy to offer this book to you and I have great satisfaction knowing that I am helping a large number of people break free of the grid and develop a home that is more sustainable and independent of the ties that entrap. I hope you send me a picture of your home as you complete it and let me know any information that you think would be helpful to include in later editions of this book.

Thank you for your interest and support. May you be blessed in the work of your hands.

Steve Rees

Made in the USA
San Bernardino, CA
18 August 2016